source to resource

FROM
RAINDROP
TO TAP

MICHAEL BRIGHT

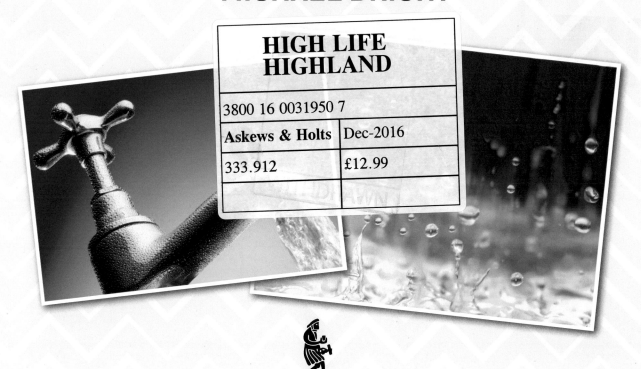

WAYLAND
www.waylandbooks.co.uk

Contents

Essential water

About 70 per cent of the surface of the Earth is **water**. It forms all the world's **oceans**, lakes and rivers, as well as the **glaciers** and ice caps. It can be found in the **clouds** and drops to the ground in **raindrops**. We can use the Earth's water sources to water our gardens, **clean ourselves** and even **warm** our homes.

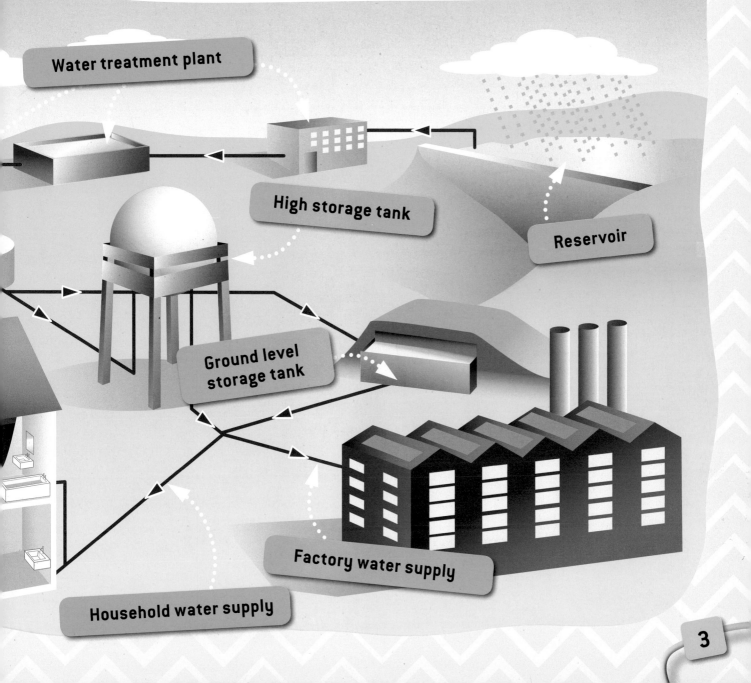

Water treatment plant

High storage tank

Reservoir

Ground level storage tank

Factory water supply

Household water supply

The blue planet

Water is essential for life on Earth and it is what makes our planet so special. Seen from space, Earth looks like a bright blue, watery planet covered with wispy clouds. It is the only planet we currently know of with liquid water on its surface.

What is water?

Water is a tasteless, colourless, transparent fluid. It is found in three forms: liquid, solid or gas. At room temperature, it is a liquid. Cool it down and it becomes solid ice. Warm it to a high temperature and it changes to an invisible gas called water vapour.

Water from space

Scientists believe that some of the Earth's water could have come from space. Very early in the Earth's history, large numbers of space rocks hit our planet. These asteroids, comets and meteorites brought with them all sorts of chemicals, including those that make water.

Asteroids, like asteroid Vesta, may have brought some of Earth's water.

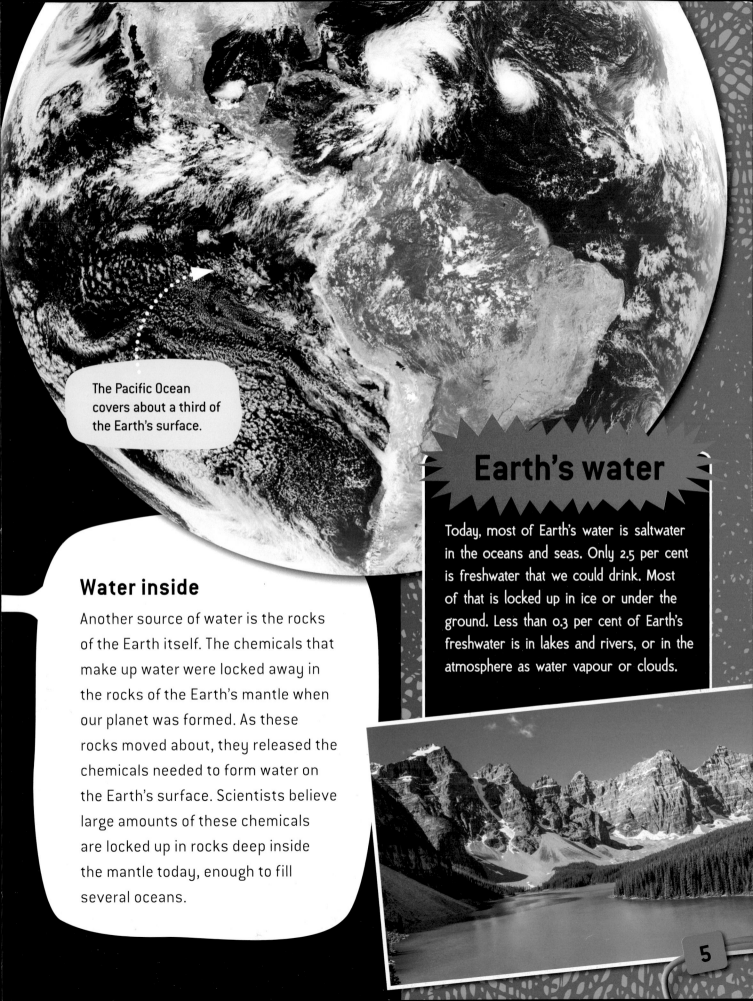

The Pacific Ocean covers about a third of the Earth's surface.

Earth's water

Today, most of Earth's water is saltwater in the oceans and seas. Only 2.5 per cent is freshwater that we could drink. Most of that is locked up in ice or under the ground. Less than 0.3 per cent of Earth's freshwater is in lakes and rivers, or in the atmosphere as water vapour or clouds.

Water inside

Another source of water is the rocks of the Earth itself. The chemicals that make up water were locked away in the rocks of the Earth's mantle when our planet was formed. As these rocks moved about, they released the chemicals needed to form water on the Earth's surface. Scientists believe large amounts of these chemicals are locked up in rocks deep inside the mantle today, enough to fill several oceans.

BRAINY BITS

The water cycle

Earth's water is continually on the move and constantly changing between being a liquid, gas or solid. The amount of water on Earth remains fairly constant, but the amount locked up in ice, flowing in lakes and rivers or carried in the atmosphere varies. The movement of water between these places and the changes it makes is known as the 'water cycle'.

5. Rain and snow
The water droplets in clouds eventually become too heavy and they fall out of the sky. If it is warm, they drop as rain. If it is cold, they drop as snow or sleet. Hail drops from thunderclouds.

6. Snowmelt
Snow and ice collects on the land, sometimes in glaciers high on icy, cold mountains. The glacier moves downhill and eventually the ice melts to liquid water and forms streams.

8. Reservoirs
Some streams flow into ponds and some rivers flow into lakes.

7. Run-off
Rain that has fallen flows downhill, first in streams, and then in rivers. Some soaks into the ground and may emerge as springs.

9. Back to the sea
Eventually, the water in rivers flows back to the sea, and the cycle starts all over again.

4. Winds

Winds blow the clouds across the ocean towards the land.

3. Clouds

The water vapour is carried up by hot air into the atmosphere. Here, it cools and changes back to its liquid form as tiny droplets of water attached to dust particles. These gather together as clouds.

Plants make the weather

Green plants have their own water cycle. Their roots take up water from the ground, and the water travels up through the plant to the leaves. It evaporates from the leaves, a process known as transpiration, and rises up into the atmosphere to form clouds. The clouds drop rain on to the ground, which is taken in by plants and the cycle starts again. It is most evident in tropical rainforests. The trees move so much water they actually create their own weather and cause a downpour almost every day.

2. Evaporation

Heat from the Sun warms the seas and oceans and the surface water turns from a liquid to the gas water vapour. The change is called evaporation.

1. Oceans

Most of the Earth's water is in the oceans.

Water and the weather

Winds circling weather systems bring us rain. Each system centres on an area of high or low atmospheric pressure, known as a 'high' or 'low'. Atmospheric pressure is the force pushing down on the Earth's surface by the weight of the atmosphere. In warm places, hot air rises so the pressure underneath is low. Cold air sinks so the pressure is high. Highs and lows move across the globe, highs bringing settled weather and lows stormy weather.

Weather fronts

Weather fronts are invisible boundaries between warm and cold parts of the atmosphere, and they also move along with the highs and lows. A warm front moves ahead of an area of warm air and a cold front in front of cold air. Most rain tends to fall just ahead of a warm front and just behind a cold front.

Clouds and weather fronts

Clouds form along weather fronts, and they appear in a particular order as the front approaches. The first signs are high cirrus and stratus clouds. Next, the first altostratus and altocumulus clouds arrive indicating the front and its rain are not far away. When big nimbus and giant cumulus clouds appear, the rain starts to fall.

On weather charts a warm front is shown as a red line with semi-circles, and a cold front as a blue line with triangles.

A monsoon is a weather system that drops lots of rain on places like India.

Cloud spotter's guide

High-level clouds

Cirrocumulus clouds are fluffy, cotton-wool-like cloudlets that indicate fair weather. They sometimes look like fish scales.

Cirrus clouds are wispy. One type is called mare's tails.

Cumulonimbus is a gigantic cloud that forms from close to the ground up to 10 km in the air, and is full of energy. Watch out for thunderstorms!

Mid-level clouds

Altocumulus appears as patches in settled weather, and waves when bad weather is coming.

Altostratus is a thin layer of cloud without features, but it indicates a storm could be on its way.

Low-level clouds

Stratocumulus is a fluffy, rounded cloud that appears in lines or waves, which can deliver light rain or snow.

Stratus is a featureless cloud that blankets everything in white or grey, sometimes with drizzle.

Cumulus is a hill-shaped cloud. When the top is cauliflower-like, heavy showers are likely.

Natural water sources

After rain has fallen from the clouds it hits the ground. The ground soaks up some of the water, especially where there are lots of trees and other plant growth that help retain it. The rest flows downhill, first into streams and then into rivers.

Hidden water

All rainwater that seeps into the ground is called groundwater. Groundwater is less likely to be polluted than water on the surface, so is often used for drinking water, either pumped up from wells or collected from natural springs. In the United States of America (USA), groundwater is the largest source of freshwater. There is more of it than all the surface lakes and man-made reservoirs put together.

Underground water

Groundwater seeps down through the rocks and can be trapped deep below the surface in porous rock, in cracks and in layers of sand, gravel or silt.

These natural underground reservoirs are known as aquifers. Even such a dry place as the Sahara has vast quantities of water deep below the desert. Wells can be drilled down to the aquifer and the water pumped up to supply people with fresh drinking water.

Spring water is often clean and safe to drink.

How aquifers work

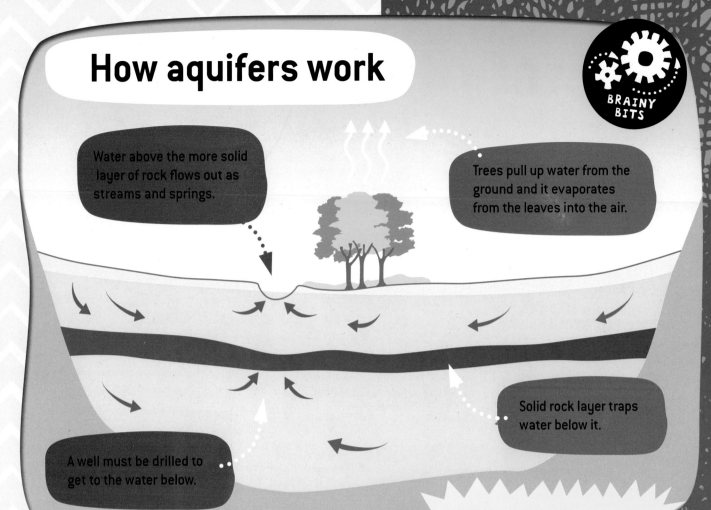

Water above the more solid layer of rock flows out as streams and springs.

Trees pull up water from the ground and it evaporates from the leaves into the air.

Solid rock layer traps water below it.

A well must be drilled to get to the water below.

Water under pressure

The layers of rocks that form these aquifers might be shaped like a bowl. Water drains towards its centre. If the level of the water in the sides of the bowl is above a well drilled in the centre, then gravity forces water up to the surface without having to pump it. These natural bowls are called artesian basins, and the well is an artesian well.

Natural dam

At 567 metres high, the Usoi Dam in Tajikistan is the world's highest natural dam. It was not built by people, but was formed in 1911 after an earthquake caused a huge quantity of rocks to fall and block the Murghab River, creating Lake Sarez.

Storing water

While nature provides many natural sources of water, man-made dams are also sources of water. Dams are built across rivers, trapping water in huge artificial lakes. Huge areas of countryside are flooded behind the dam, sometimes including towns and villages.

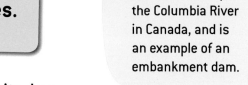

The Mica Dam spans the Columbia River in Canada, and is an example of an embankment dam.

Dam design

There are several types of dam, each designed not to collapse under the weight of water building up behind.

Arch dam

Made of concrete, the arch dam is curved towards the lake it holds back. It is designed so that the pressure of water behind strengthens the dam. It is most often used across gorges and canyons.

Gravity dam

A gravity dam is made of strong materials, such as concrete and stone, that can hold back the enormous weight of the water building up behind it.

Embankment dam

Made from compacted earth or rocks, the side facing the lake is usually lined with concrete or masonry. It works like a gravity dam.

The Contra Dam in Switzerland is a thin, curved arch dam.

The Hoover Dam, on the Arizona-Nevada border in the USA, is an example of a gravity dam.

Low dams and weirs

Low dams and weirs are placed across rivers to restrict but not stop their flow. Water behind the dam or weir can be diverted to the water supply system.

Flooded wildlife

The world's biggest man-made reservoir is Lake Kariba on the border of Zambia and Zimbabwe. When the Kariba Dam was constructed, wildlife had to be rescued from the rising waters and released elsewhere.

DID YOU KNOW?

The world's highest man-made dam is the Jinping-1 Dam in China. It is 305 metres tall.

Electricity from water

A by-product of storing water behind dams is hydroelectric power. It is the most widely used form of renewable energy, with more than 16 per cent of the world's electricity generated this way.

How does it work?

Hydroelectricity generation depends on gravity. Water from the reservoir is channelled into the power station. Here, the falling or rushing water turns the propeller-like fans of a water turbine before the water heads out to sea. The turbine is linked to a generator. When the turbine turns the generator, it produces electricity. This electricity is then transported along electricity cables to reach the national grid.

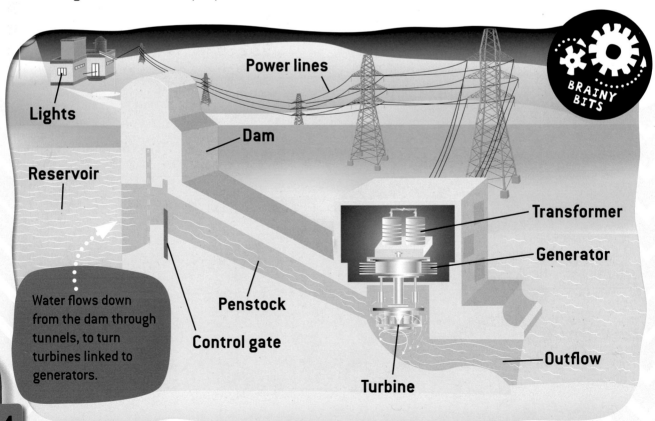

Lights

Power lines

Dam

Reservoir

Transformer

Generator

Water flows down from the dam through tunnels, to turn turbines linked to generators.

Penstock

Control gate

Turbine

Outflow

BRAINY BITS

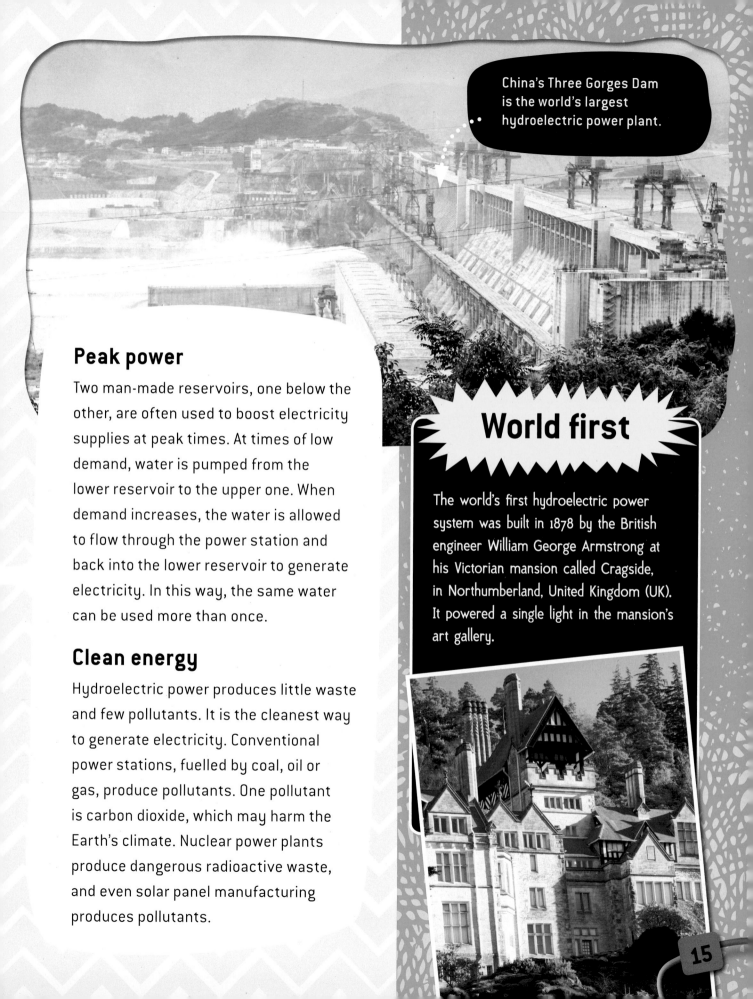

China's Three Gorges Dam is the world's largest hydroelectric power plant.

Peak power

Two man-made reservoirs, one below the other, are often used to boost electricity supplies at peak times. At times of low demand, water is pumped from the lower reservoir to the upper one. When demand increases, the water is allowed to flow through the power station and back into the lower reservoir to generate electricity. In this way, the same water can be used more than once.

Clean energy

Hydroelectric power produces little waste and few pollutants. It is the cleanest way to generate electricity. Conventional power stations, fuelled by coal, oil or gas, produce pollutants. One pollutant is carbon dioxide, which may harm the Earth's climate. Nuclear power plants produce dangerous radioactive waste, and even solar panel manufacturing produces pollutants.

World first

The world's first hydroelectric power system was built in 1878 by the British engineer William George Armstrong at his Victorian mansion called Cragside, in Northumberland, United Kingdom (UK). It powered a single light in the mansion's art gallery.

Water treatment

While underground water can be drunk directly from clean wells and springs, the surface water from reservoirs, lakes and rivers is usually treated before it is used as drinking water. Water treatment plants can be built close to a dam, or some distance away on the outskirts of a city.

Roman water systems

Today, water is generally moved about in enclosed pipes, but the ancient Romans created extensive systems of open aqueducts, man-made channels that carry water. The channels followed the slopes of the land, relying on water flowing downhill. Over valleys, the aqueducts were carried on special bridges. At the edge of the city, the water poured into tanks in which sediments settled out before the clean water was distributed to households, much like modern water treatment facilities do.

Ancient Roman aqueduct Pont du Gard, near Nîmes, southern France.

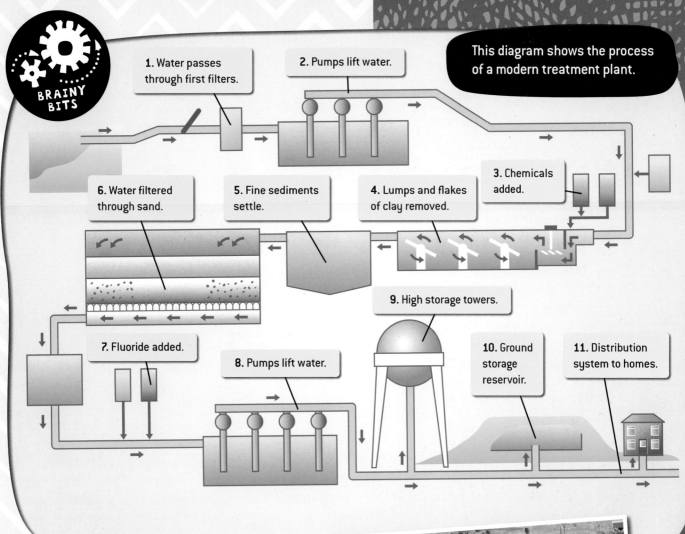

This diagram shows the process of a modern treatment plant.

1. Water passes through first filters.

2. Pumps lift water.

3. Chemicals added.

4. Lumps and flakes of clay removed.

5. Fine sediments settle.

6. Water filtered through sand.

7. Fluoride added.

8. Pumps lift water.

9. High storage towers.

10. Ground storage reservoir.

11. Distribution system to homes.

Modern water treatment

Today, water destined for the household tap is treated at the water treatment plant. Gritty sediments settle out in big tanks and smaller debris is filtered out. Adding chemicals, such as chlorine, to the water, kills bacteria. Adding fluoride helps tackle tooth decay, especially in children. In most developed countries, the treated water is then pumped into towns and cities along complex networks of pipes.

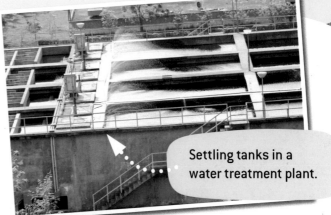

Settling tanks in a water treatment plant.

DID YOU KNOW?

The word 'plumber' comes from the Latin 'plumbum', meaning 'lead'. In ancient Rome, a plumber was somebody who worked with lead.

Water for the home

Water generally reaches a home through large pipes under the street, known as 'water mains'. The water running through them is at high pressure. Outside each house, a pressure reducer lowers the pressure before the water enters the house. This lower pressure makes sure the water comes out of the tap at a steady rate.

Safety valve

At some point between the water main and the household supply is a special valve, called a 'stopcock'. If there is a leak in the house, the valve can be closed and the water supply cut off before it makes too much mess.

A stopcock controls the flow of water through the pipes.

Water in the house

Inside the house, cold water pipes deliver water to cold water taps. When you turn on a tap, a screw with a leather or rubber washer lifts from the end of the water pipe and the water flows. When you turn it off, the screw pushes the washer down and onto the end of the water pipe, blocking the water flow.

Cold water also goes to shower heaters, toilets and a boiler, which warms the water and delivers hot water to hot water taps. A further branch feeds the central heating system, in which water is warmed and sent to radiators around the house.

Water squirts up under high pressure from a burst water main.

Water towers

In places where the land is particularly flat, water is often pumped up into a large water tower, where it is stored. Pipes link the tower to homes, and gravity does the rest. It provides enough pressure to ensure the water flows freely out of the tap.

Hard and soft water

Drinking water can be 'hard' or 'soft'. Its hardness depends on the rocks over which it has flowed. Hard water is found in limestone and chalk country, such as the Pennines, UK. It contains high levels of the chemical calcium, which can leave a white deposit inside kitchen appliances, such as kettles, making them less efficient. Soft water is found where the rocks are granite or sandstone, such as Dartmoor, UK. It does not leave a deposit. Soft water readily forms lather with soap, but with hard water this is more difficult.

Kuwait Water Towers are part of a modern water system built for Kuwait City.

Water at work

Water is also used outside the home. Industry uses it to help in the manufacturing process of a whole range of products. Farming the land also requires a large amount of water.

When the temperature is 10 °C, cows drink 23 litres of water a day – and much more when it is warmer.

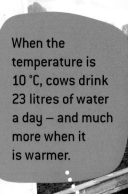

Farm water

Agriculture accounts for about 70 per cent of the freshwater used by people worldwide. The water is mainly used to irrigate crops. Without it, farmers would be unable to grow the food or raise the animals needed to feed the world's growing population.

Watering crops

Irrigation has been important for as long as people have been farming. At first, buckets would have been used to carry water to crops. Later civilisations, such as the ancient Egyptians, soon used irrigation channels. Today, all sorts of irrigation techniques are used.

In dry places, farmers have moving spray water guns on long arms that rotate around a central water supply.

Factory water

Almost every manufacturing process uses water in some way. It can be used for cooling machinery, washing, diluting or dissolving chemicals, transporting, or can be used within the product itself. Industries that require large quantities of water, such as paper and steel production, tend not to use the public supply but have their own small, self-contained reservoirs.

Steam from cooling towers and chimneys shows how much water a factory uses.

Aquaculture

Large tanks of water are required to farm freshwater fish, such as tilapia. Farm-raised fish, such as trout, are bred in tanks to be released into lakes for anglers to catch, and farmed fish are also available in local supermarkets for us to buy and eat.

A fish farm located in the countryside of Thailand.

Hydro-burgers!

It might come as a surprise to find that enormous quantities of water are required to make things that do not seem very 'watery'. The growing and making of a single quarter-pound hamburger, for example, requires about 2,045 litres of water! It takes large quantities of water to grow the crops to feed the cow. Then, there is the water for the cow to drink, and the water to keep it clean, and a large amount of water is involved during the making of the hamburger itself.

Water use in the home

Water companies make sure that clean water reaches homes, yet only a small amount of that water is actually drunk. The rest is used in other household activities, such as washing.

It is important to drink plenty of water every day.

My water 'footprint'

In countries with adequate water supplies, such as the UK and the USA, everyone uses about 150 litres of water a day. If the quantity of water used by agriculture and the food industry is added to this, along with all the other products we use that require water in their manufacture, the figure rises to a staggering 3,400 litres a day.

Where does all our water go?

Of all the drinkable water that is supplied to the home, only 4 per cent is actually drunk as drinking water. The rest is used for all sorts of household tasks, and as much as a third is just flushed away.

Drinking water is used for many things other than drinking.

Personal washing 33%

Toilet flushing 30%

Clothes washing 13%

Watering the garden and cleaning the car 7%

Washing up dishes 8%

Other uses 5%

Add up your average daily water consumption

Copy this water consumption chart on to a piece of paper.

Fill it in every day and add up how much water you use in a week.

Daily activity	Average usage	Uses per week	x No. of people in household	Weekly total in litres
Bath	80 litres per bath	x ( )	x ( )	= ( )
Standard shower	45 litres per 5 min shower	x ( )	x ( )	= ( )
Power shower	75 litres per 5 min shower	x ( )	x ( )	= ( )
Toilet flush	7.5 litres per flush	x ( )	x ( )	= ( )
Teeth cleaning (with taps running)	6 litres per clean	x ( )	x ( )	= ( )
Hand/face wash	2 litres per clean	x ( )	x ( )	= ( )

Daily activity	Average usage	Uses per week	Weekly total in litres
Washing machine	85 litres per load	x ( )	= ( )
Dishwasher	42 litres per load	x ( )	= ( )
Food preparation	15 litres per occasion	x ( )	= ( )
Washing up by hand	15 litres per occasion	x ( )	= ( )
Total use of water by your household			= ( )
Divide by 7 for daily consumption			= ( )
Divide by number of people to find each person's average			= ( )
Add 25 litres for miscellaneous water uses			= ( )
Total average daily water consumption per person			= ( )

How does your water consumption compare with the 150 litres per day national average?

23

How to save water

People in countries with a good water supply tend to take water for granted. They turn on the tap and out it flows. It means large quantities are wasted. It can be wasted in all sorts of ways, even from damaged water mains and other leaks in the system. However, people at home can help to save water.

Here are some tips...

- Turn off the tap when brushing your teeth. It wastes more than 6 litres per minute.

- Fix a dripping tap. It can waste about 60 litres of water a week.

- Short showers, of about 4 minutes, are less wasteful than baths. A bath uses about 80 litres of water, while a shower uses a third of that, except power showers that can use more water than a bath.

- A displacement device fitted in an older type of toilet cistern reduces the volume of water used in each flush.

- Fill a jug with water and place it in the fridge overnight, so you do not have to run the tap in the morning to get a cold drink.

- Fill the kettle with just the amount of water you need for your tea or coffee.

Make sure a dishwasher or washing machine is full before starting it. Choose the 'economy' or 'eco-option' cycle.

24

- Wash fruit and vegetables in a bowl and not under the running tap.

- Water the garden with a watering can and not a hose, and water in the early morning or evening.

- Install a water meter. Knowing and being charged for the exact amount of water you use might be an incentive to not waste it.

Free water

One way to save water is to have your own mini-reservoir. You can harvest rainwater by having a water butt fed by the downpipe that carries water off the roof of your house.

Remember to turn the tap off while you brush your teeth.

DID YOU KNOW?
In hot, dry weather, up to half of the water used 'per person' is actually sprinkled on the garden!

Drinking water

People need to drink clean water in order to live healthy lives. Water flushes out dangerous chemicals from your vital organs, carries nutrients to your cells and generally helps keep your body working properly. Lack of water can lead to dehydration.

Water for health

It is often said that a healthy person should drink about eight glasses of water per day, but no single formula fits everybody. Even so, health authorities suggest that two to three litres of fluids a day, to include water and beverages, is beneficial.

Active people

Children who do activities such as swimming and football, as well as athletes, need more water to replace that lost by sweating. Similarly, active people in hot countries need more water, up to 16 litres a day in extreme cases.

Clean, fresh water is essential for good health.

People who do lots of exercise need to drink water more regularly.

About 65 per cent of the human body is water. A newborn baby can be as much as 75 per cent water, while an elderly person can be as little as 45 per cent water.

Where does our body water come from?

Water straight from the tap is not our only source. We get water from foods that are made up largely of water. The water content of foods can vary, but on average: drinking water accounts for about 30 per cent of a person's water intake; beverages, such as tea and coffee, account for 45 per cent; and food 25 per cent.

Butter
15
per cent
water

Tomato
94
per cent
water

Bread
35
per cent
water

Milk
87
per cent
water

Boiled
egg
73
per cent
water

Tea and
coffee
99
per cent
water

Clean water for everyone

There are more than seven billion people in the world, of which a billion have no access to clean drinking water. Two million of them die each year from diseases contracted from contaminated water.

Drinking water from the sea

Desalination is the process of removing salt from saltwater to make freshwater. With droughts more likely in the future, desalination could help with water shortages, but it requires a lot of electricity. In Europe, it is used to top up water supplies, but in the Middle East many countries depend on it.

The good news

In 2000, the United Nations tasked all its members to halve the number of people who do not have clean water by 2015. This was achieved five years early, when over 2 billion more people had drinking water in 2010 than in 1990.

The bad news

Although nearly 90 per cent of people worldwide have access to clean drinking water, this leaves more than 10 per cent who do not. Many live in areas without piped water or sewers. They collect their water from open pits and ponds, and it is contaminated by sewage. Terrible diseases, such as cholera, are common.

This man's only water supply is a dirty river.

A women pumps water from a public well in Tanzania.

The better news

Solar water disinfection has been introduced in some poor countries. This technology uses energy from the Sun. By focusing sunlight on the water container using mirrors, the water can be boiled, killing harmful bacteria. This has been shown to reduce the number of water-borne diseases by 80 per cent.

Not on tap

In places without modern water systems and where natural disasters have struck, such as earthquakes, serious flooding or prolonged drought, water is often delivered in road tankers. People must come to the distribution point with cans and water bottles in order to take home enough water for them to survive another day.

Basic right

The charity Water Aid states that: "everyone, everywhere needs a safe and sustainable supply of water: for drinking, washing, cleaning, cooking and growing food. It's a basic human right." The challenge is to achieve this. But in the future, the increasing world population means the demand for fresh, clean drinking water is likely to exceed the supply. Then every country, no matter how wealthy, could be facing water shortages.

The water from the tanker is clean compared to any obtained from a local pond or river.

Glossary

asteroid A small, rocky body that orbits the Sun

atmosphere The layer of air surrounding the Earth

atmospheric pressure The pressure exerted by the weight of air in the atmosphere

beverage A drink other than water

canyon A narrow valley with steep cliff walls

cholera A dangerous disease of the small intestine caused by bacteria, often found in dirty water

comet A small space body of ice and rock that sometimes has a 'tail'

compacted When something is packed tightly together

dehydration The huge loss of water from the body

disinfect To cleanse something and kill any bacteria in it

generator A machine that makes electricity

gorge A deep, narrow valley with very steep sides

gravity The force that causes objects to fall to the ground or water to flow downhill

hail Falling pellets of ice

hydroelectricity Electricity generated using the movement of water

ice cap A dome-shaped covering of ice over the land

irrigate To supply water to farmland by sprinklers, ditches or channels

lather A foam made with soap and water

mantle The layer of the Earth between the central core and the outer crust

masonry Stonework or brickwork

meteorite A stony or metallic object that falls to Earth from outer space

pollutant A waste product that makes air or water harmful

porous Describes something that allows the passage of gases and liquids, like a sponge

radioactive Describes something that gives off dangerous rays

renewable Describes something that never runs out

sediment A material that settles to the bottom of a liquid

sewer A drain or pipe that takes away waste water from the house and rainwater from the street

sleet Pellets of melting snowflakes or freezing raindrops

spring A natural source of water flowing out of the ground

transparent Describes something that can be seen through

water butt A barrel-shaped container used to collect rainwater

water turbine A machine with a propellor-like wheel that is turned by the movement of water

water vapour The gas phase of water

Further information

BOOKS

Can the Earth Cope? Water Supply
by Louise Spilsbury, Wayland 2013

Earth Cycles: Water
by Sally Morgan, Franklin Watts 2012

Environment Detective Investigates: Saving Water
by Jen Green, Wayland 2010

World Energy Issues: Water Power – Is It Efficient?
by Jim Pope, Franklin Watts 2010

WEBSITES

Go here for fun facts about water:
http://www.sciencekids.co.nz/sciencefacts/water.html

The BBC Bitesize webpage will give you lots of information about water energy:
http://www.bbc.co.uk/schools/gcsebitesize/science/aqa_pre_2011/energy/mainselectricityrev4.shtml

More facts about why it is important to save water:
http://www.waterwise.org.uk/pages/why-we-need-to-save-water.html

Index

First published in Great Britain in 2016 by Wayland
Copyright © Wayland, 2016

All rights reserved.

Author: Michael Bright
Freelance editor: Katie Woolley
Editors: Annabel Stones and Liza Miller
Designer: Rocket Design (East Anglia) Ltd

ISBN: 9780750296502
10 9 8 7 6 5 4 3 2 1

Wayland
An imprint of
Hachette Children's Group
Part of Hodder & Stoughton
Carmelite House
50 Victoria Embankment
London EC4Y 0DZ

An Hachette UK Company
www.hachette.co.uk
www.hachettechildrens.co.uk

Printed in China

Illustrations by Stefan Chabluk: 2–3, 8, 9, 11t, 17

Picture credits:
All images and graphic elements courtesy of
Shutterstock except:
4: NASA. 11b: Jonathan Renouf/Alamy. 12t:
Dave Blackey/All Canada Photos/Corbis. 15b:
Jason Friend/Loop Images/Corbis. 18:
Pratchaya Leelapatchayanont/Dreamstime. 19b:
Typhoonski/Dreamstime. 21t:
Kevin Wilton/Eye Ubiquitous/Corbis.

Every effort has been made to clear copyright.
Should there be any inadvertent omission, please
apply to the publisher for rectification.

The website addresses (URLs) included in this
book were valid at the time of going to press.
However, it is possible that contents or addresses
may have changed since the publication of this
book. No responsibility for any such changes can
be accepted by either the author or the Publisher.

source to resource

The four books in the Source to Resource series examine Earth's most important resources. They support the geography curriculum and are designed to encourage readers to debate some of today's most pressing environmental issues.

FROM FIELD TO PLATE

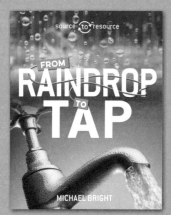

MICHAEL BRIGHT

978 0 7502 9645 8

FROM OIL RIG TO PETROL PUMP

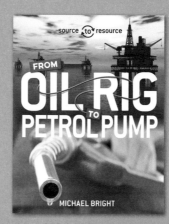

MICHAEL BRIGHT

978 0 7502 9648 9

FROM RAINDROP TO TAP

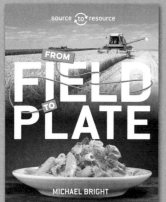

MICHAEL BRIGHT

978 0 7502 9650 2

FROM SUNSHINE TO LIGHTBULB

MICHAEL BRIGHT

978 0 7502 9649 6